Seize Your Greatness

Harnessing Passion and Purpose

Table of Contents

The two most important days in your life are the day you are born and the day you find out why.

— Mark Twain

Chapter 1. Introduction

Let the journey to the best version of yourself begin! Our Special Report, "Seize Your Greatness: Harnessing Passion and Purpose," dives into the invigorating world of self-discovery, determination, and the raw power of finding your inherent strengths. Imagine waking up every day, brimming with a profound sense of purpose, and being driven by a passion that fuels your desire to reach unprecedented heights. This is not just another report; it is a transformative expedition, a beacon of positivity and perseverance every step of the way. Reading this report is an investment not in a product, but in your life's most crucial project - you. So why wait? Seize your greatness, discover your unparalleled potential, and let's take this remarkable journey together to a vibrant horizon shimmering with possibilities!

Chapter 2. Unveiling Your True Self

This journey begins with stepping onto an inward path that leads to the revelation of your authentic, radiant, and dynamic self! This exploratory expedition places a powerful magnet to your inner compass as you venture into the uncharted territories of your soul. Regular introspection, self-correction, and the courage to embrace your vulnerabilities are your guiding beacons throughout this journey. There are no signboards or preset routes here; in fact, the destination itself constantly evolves, growing in tandem with your understanding of your true self.

2.1. The Journey Inward

Many embark on this journey, hastening towards a perceived semblance of the 'ideal self'. However, the pursuit of such a self can be likened to chasing the horizon. It's not about molding ourselves into archetypes prescribed by society. Such external constructs limit the vast canvas of potential, hindering the possibility of discovering who we truly are. Now is the time for you to step out of these molds. Disentangling from these external constraints, we must dare to dive deeply into our inner universe.

Make a distinct turn towards introspection. This is not a leisurely stroll but a feat that requires courage and honesty. The light you will hold while navigating the nooks and crannies of your internal terrain will be your courage, and your truthful reflection will guide the exploration.

Upon entering the labyrinth of our inner worlds, one notably encounters the Ego, which invariably casts imposing, elongated shadows on the realms of our true selves. It can be a daunting task to separate our ego's constructs from our authentic selves. Yet, this is where the real journey begins - the path where we confront these shadows and strive to make peace with them.

2.2. Emotional Intelligence and Self Awareness

An essential tool for this inward journey is emotional intelligence, which primarily comprises self-awareness and self-regulation. It empowers you to comprehend the depth and complexity of your own emotions, helping you manage and harness them effectively. These skills are invaluable when venturing into our inner worlds.

Exercise emotional intelligence, fortify your awareness, and you will find that your emotions can serve as fantastic signposts, helping you navigate your internal landscapes rather than being obstacles. Begin to ask intimate questions of yourself. Look past the superficial layers of your emotions and try to understand the true essence behind each feeling. Emotions can act as windows, providing glimpses into the depth of our true being.

2.3. Befriending Vulnerability

Equally important is the willingness to embrace vulnerability. Shattering the prevalent myth that vulnerability is a weakness, it is actually a profound strength. Your ability to lean into and acknowledge vulnerabilities indicates the presence of an authentic self that is willing to be seen and known in its entirety, with all its shades.

Moving towards vulnerability instead of away from it can be a transformational and healing experience. Allow yourself to risk uncertainty, expose your raw self, feel the fear, and still choose to be accepting and open. One truly impresses the marks of authenticity onto their selves when they dare to present their uncensored, unfiltered selves to their conscious perception.

2.4. Self Compassion

Wandering through the wilderness of your internal world can sometimes be heart-rending. You may meet ghosts from past mistakes, unfulfilled dreams, regrets, sorrows, and the like. To endure these emotional confrontations, self-compassion must be held dear.

Self-compassion encourages you to be kind to yourself, nurturing a friendly relationship with yourself along the journey. It suggests recognizing your humanness and providing yourself the same kindness and understanding you would extend to a close friend who is suffering. Self-compassion is ultimately what helps sustain your journey inward, ensuring that this exploration is guided by love and patience, not criticism and intolerance.

2.5. The Treasure Trove of Your True Self

After traveling through the layered landscapes of your self, as you align more with your true self, you will notice that your eyes will start recognizing a familiar glow, a warmth that comforts and a strength that empowers. This internal journey is not a quick-fix solution to existential woes; it is a perpetual, life-long process. Yet, the rewards far exceed the struggles. You will begin to forge a bond with your self so deep that it acts as an inexhaustible source of inspiration, resilience, and wisdom. This will guide your actions and decisions, influencing your external reality in profound ways.

Harnessing the power of this journey, this chapter therefore sets the foundation on which the entire structure of 'Seizing your greatness' is to be erected. Consequently, becoming an ongoing ally in your quest for becoming the best version of yourself.

Let your authentic self shine unapologetically and create a life that reverberates with the symphony of your unique essence. This dance of self-revelation, once begun with determination and purpose, will take you on a challenging but truly satisfying journey, creating an enthralling narrative of your life, ever enriching and full of unexpected joys.

Chapter 3. The Power of Passion: Igniting the Inner Flame

Passion is the divine spark, an incendiary force that, when harnessed, has the ability to transform the mundane into extraordinary. Teetering between dreams and reality, if employed pragmatically, it is an activator of unprecedented achievement and unparalleled satisfaction. This unfettered force originates from the core of our being, precipitating an ethereal chain of evocative thoughts, inspiring actions, and transformative decisions, thus laying the groundwork for an iconic journey towards the relentless pursuit of your soul's true calling.

3.1. The Genesis of Passion

Understanding the essence of passion begins with delving into the core of its genesis. Every individual is bestowed with a unique set of interests, talents, and abilities. Our passions amplify these natural tendencies, accentuating our inherent capabilities. Passion is not just a hobby or a part-time interest; it's an undying infatuation, an indomitable will, consuming your thoughts and propelling you inexorably towards its pursuit. It is crucial to introspect, to delve deep into the core of our persona, recognize what stimulates our interest, provokes our curiosity, or provides us with a sense of accomplishment. This self-awareness facilitates the identification of our passions.

3.2. Discern Between Transient Interests and True Passion

In the journey of distinguishing passion, it's essential not to confuse transient interests with true passion. To articulate the difference, transient interests are fleeting and change with time, while passion is a steady flame that grows brighter and resilient with each challenge faced. The allure of novelty might incite a transient interest, but it's the enduring allure, the unstoppable yearning even in the face of adversity that signifies true passion. Take note of repeating patterns, the activities that not only hold your attention but also give you contentment. Keep a close eye and cherish the experiences that invigorate you, for they might be harboring your true passion.

3.3. Nurturing Your Passion

Once you have uncovered your passion, the nurturing phase begins. It's analogous to tending to a young sapling, providing it with the right balance of sunlight, water, and nutrients for it to thrive. Similarly, your passion requires an optimum mix of time, effort and perseverance to flourish. Submerge yourself in the realms of your passion, learn, evolve, experiment, fall, and rise again. This cyclical process of iterative learning and unlearning will guide you to mastery. Subscribe to courses, attend seminars, read books or seek mentorship - whatever your chosen path, pursue it with unwavering determination.

3.4. Transforming Passion into Purpose

The transformation of passion into purpose is the inflection point in the journey towards actualizing one's potential. This requires not just identifying and nurturing your passion, but aligning it with your life's overarching goals. It's about channeling the energy of your passion to serve a higher purpose that transcends your individual existence. It could involve transforming your passion into a meaningful profession, or using your passion as a springboard to effect positive change in society. This transformation holds the promise of a life lived with fervor, fulfillment, and in resonance with your higher self.

3.5. Life With Passion Versus Life Without Passion

Life without passion is like a song devoid of melody. It is a monotonous existence, stripped bare of the vibrant colors of creativity and excitement. On the contrary, a passion-led life is intrinsically rewarding and characteristically vibrant. It widens our perceptive lens, offering a unique life experience punctuated by periods of deep engagement and meaningful growth. It fuels intrinsic motivation, instigates perseverance, fosters resilience, and engenders a sense of accomplishment.

In conclusion, awakening the power of your passion entails understanding its origin, differentiating it from transient interests, fostering its growth, and transforming it into a purpose. Passion, when ignited and integrated aptly into the fabric of your life, can elevate your existence from mediocrity to magnanimity, from simple survival to transcendental thriving. As we conclude this chapter, reconnect with your intrinsic interests, and dare to fan the flames of your inner passion. For it's only when you don the suit of courage to hunt, negotiate, and seize your life's untamed wild passions that you embark on the authentic journey to becoming the best version of your true self.

Chapter 4. Crafting Your Personal Vision: A Blueprint to Purpose

To understand the magnitude of crafting your personal vision, we must first grapple with the notion of what personal vision actually entails. Simply put, personal vision is the forward-looking view of what you aspire to achieve or become. It acts as a guiding light, assisting you in making decisions that align with your spiritual purpose and personal goals. It's the framework, the blueprint according to which all revolutions in life are instigated.

4.1. The Importance of Personal Vision

Personal vision is pivotal for leading a purposeful life. It enlightens us about our core values, aspirations, and ambitions, helping carve a systematic path towards self-fulfillment. Personal vision, like a compass, guides us to our chosen destination, despite the distractions and disruptions that may attempt to veil our course. It also influences our behavior, shapes our attitudes, and plays an important role in determining the people we let into our lives. Without a defined vision, our undertakings might become rudderless, making it exceedingly difficult to anchor in the stormy seas of life's challenges.

4.2. Generating Your Personal Vision

Crafting your personal vision is not a one-size-fits-all process; it varies from person to person, depending on individual interests, propensities, experiences, and aspirations. To start off, set aside some quiet time for introspection. Reflect on what kindles joy, fulfillment, and passion within you. Ask yourself questions related to your interests, long-terms goals, life's ambitions, talents, and personal values. Jot down your thoughts, experiences, and aspirations. Let it flow naturally, without editing or analyzing. This brainstorming is the very first step towards shaping your personal vision.

4.3. Clearing The Vision

After the brainstorming session, start analyzing and organizing your thoughts. Identify patterns, recurring themes, values, and goals that emerge from your reflections. This will help in establishing the core components of your personal vision. At this juncture, you may also want to consider any constraints or elephants in the room. Understandably, these limitations could influence the pace, but remember, they need not derail the journey. They should be considered not as roadblocks, but challenges that might require innovative solutions.

4.4. Creating Your Personal Vision Statement

Your personal vision statement serves as a written affirmation of your desired future. It acts as both a driver and a yardstick, propelling you forward while simultaneously measuring your progress. The sooner you start penning down your personal vision statement, the better. Be specific, be honest, and most importantly - be you! The statement should resonate with who you are and what you genuinely aspire to become. Keep it handy, so you can revisit and reassess it periodically, adjusting as you evolve.

4.5. Cultivating Commitment and Consistency

A vision without dedicated commitment is akin to a high-performance car without fuel. For the vision to come to life, constant, conscientious efforts are required. Consistency leads to habit formation, and these habits, in turn, dramatically influence personal and professional victories. So, be relentless in the journey of achieving your vision, cultivating a resolve that withstands the fiercest of life's tempests.

4.6. Building Vision Alignment

Your personal vision serves no purpose if your daily actions don't reflect it. Thus, ensure that your actions air in harmony with your vision. They should represent your mission, contributing to its attainment. This alignment not only speeds up the process of actualizing your vision but also boosts self-motivation and a sense of fulfillment.

4.7. The Power of Visualization

Visualization is a dynamic and effective tool that bolsters the journey towards your vision's materialization. It involves imagining, in vivid detail, the accomplishment of your goals. It stimulates the subconscious mind, setting in motion a series of events that guide you closer towards your end goals. Make visualization a part of your routine, letting it serve as a daily reminder of your vision and its glorious destination.

Crafting a personal vision can be an enlightening and transformative experience, offering you the remarkable opportunity to design the life you aspire to lead. It's the first step towards unforgettable adventures and a fulfilling existence. Remember, what seems but a mere dream today, with a keen vision, unwavering commitment and enduring consistency, could morph into a captivating reality tomorrow. Embrace this journey and paint the canvas of your life with vibrant hues of purpose and passion!

Chapter 5. Building Resilience: Overcoming Life's Obstacles

The concept of resilience rings with an air of invincibility. Like an enduring river stone that simply allows the rapids to wash over it, resilience encapsulates the ability to persistently tackle adversity head-on, weather the storm and emerge stronger. As we delve into this dense, transformative terrain of building resilience in this chapter, we shall uncover the techniques and strategies to navigate life's ceaseless whirlwinds with grace and fortitude.

5.1. Unraveling The Essence of Resilience

Resilience is not about refusing to fall, but about the courage and strength to rise each time we stumble. It's about developing an unrelinquished will to dance in the face of adversity, inspiring oneself to turn trials into triumphs. But how can this resilience be developed? It lies in the intricate balance between understanding our emotional reactions, amplifying positive thinking, fostering healthy relationships, setting realistic life goals, and imbuing absolute self-belief.

5.2. Embracing Emotional Agility

To cultivate resilience, we must first embrace our emotional range. Struggles, disappointments, and heartbreaks are as much a part of the human experience as joy, love, and success. Emotional agility involves observing our feelings without judgement, allowing ourselves to fully experience them, and then taking mindful actions aligned with our core values. By engaging in emotional agility, we adapt to stressors, disrupt negative patterns, and pivot towards a more balanced, resilient way of living.

5.3. Cultivating Positive Psychology

Studies have accentuated the role of positive psychology in building resilience. Positive psychology focuses on fostering positive emotions, nurturing personal strengths, promoting a sense of purpose, and generating a reservoir of hope. It emphasizes gratitude, mindfulness, and optimism as potent tools to rebound from setbacks and keep moving forward. Empirical studies suggest a clear correlation between the propensity for experiencing positive emotions and the ability to bounce back from adversity.

5.4. Establishing Realistic Goal Setting

To become resilient, one must learn to recognize their own limitations and potential, establishing goals that are adequately challenging yet achievable. One approach is the SMART method, which entails creating goals that are Specific, Measurable, Achievable, Relevant, and Time-bound. Realistic goal setting boosts self-confidence and fosters resilience by continuously providing a source of motivation and a clear path forward.

5.5. Enouncing The Power of Self-Belief

Accentuating self-belief is another critical element in developing resilience, enabling us to surmount obstacles and recover from setbacks. Self-belief builds on accepting oneself 'as is,' nurturing an unwavering faith in our abilities, and consistently challenging our limits. It helps reduce anxiety, enhances optimism, and motivates us to become the architects of our desired realities.

5.6. Nurturing a Solid Support Network

Humans are social beings, hence, strong, dependable relationships can bolster our resilience. A support network does not necessarily mean a large group of people; even a handful of trusted, nurturing, and affirming relationships can provide emotional ballast during turbulent times to propel us forward. They can offer needed perspectives and resources, constituting a valuable component of any resilience-building strategy.

5.7. Leveraging The Benefits of Physical Health

Physical fitness is also directly connected to our resilience. Regular physical activity can not only aid in maintaining good health but also serve as a coping mechanism for stress and boost mood by releasing endorphins, the body's feel-good neurotransmitters.

This journey of building resilience is a trek of self-awareness, learning to embrace our emotional spectrum, adopting positive psychology, realizing realistic goals, amplifying self-belief, fostering supportive networks, and harnessing physical wellness. Each step on this path is a testament to courage and growth, a reflection of our ability to bounce back and surpass our struggles. Because beneath the turbulent currents of life lies the precious pearl of resilience that abides undeterred, bright and shining, waiting to be discovered, nurtured, and cherished by each one of us.

Chapter 6. The Art of Persistence: Journey to Mastery

A journey to mastery is never linear or swift - it's a path punctuated by roadblocks, detours, and seemingly insurmountable challenges. Just as a mountaineer's expedition to the summit is marred by blizzards, rocky terrains, and relentless fatigue, the ascent to mastery requires an extraordinary kind of courage: the courage to persist. Therefore, it's imperative to arm yourself with the art of persistence, a crucial tool that could recalibrate the way you approach your dreams and ambitions.

6.1. Unraveling the Power of Persistence

Persistence is often misinterpreted as sheer doggedness or obstinacy. On the contrary, it is the landmark of true grit, a testament to your unwavering commitment to your dreams. It resonates with stick-to-itiveness, the ability to maintain your course in the face of adversity, failure, and even crushing disillusionment. It is a personal attribute that operates in tandem with building resilience, igniting passion, and honing aptitudes. But above all, it acts as the powerful bridge connecting passion to mastery.

Understanding the rhythm of persistent efforts involves nimbly maneuvering through hurdles rather than obliterating them. As epitomized by water, which does not resist obstacles but rather, flows around them - adjusting its course yet never ceasing its journey to the ocean. Similarly, your path to self-mastery demands a 'water-like' approach: flowing, unyielding, relentless.

6.2. Nurturing a Persistent Mindset

Our minds dictate how we respond to failure and adversity. Nurturing a persistent mindset is a vital part of this narrative. One approach is affirmations: powerful, positive reinforcing statements you repeatedly tell yourself, ultimately shaping your mindset. Note that affirmations are not merely sugar-coated platitude. They should echo your true aspirations and resonate with your individual truth.

To embed affirmations in your daily life, find a quiet space, close your eyes and imagine that you have already accomplished your goal. Such visualization can be galvanized by positive affirmations, strengthening your resolve to not just dream, but to persistently work towards realizing your dream.

Another powerful strategy is to harness the power of a growth mindset. A term coined by psychologist Carol Dweck, it encourages embracing failure, not as a dead-end, but a stepping stone to success. It's a mindset that believes intelligence, talent, and skills can be developed, not innate and fixed. By maintaining a growth mindset throughout your journey to mastery, you invite an opportunity to constantly evolve, learn and grow.

6.3. The Link: GRIT and Persistence

If you peel back the layers of those who have ascended the apex of any field, you'll often discover a potent mix of passion and persistence, encapsulated in the term 'grit.' In her groundbreaking book 'Grit: The Power of Passion and Perseverance,' psychologist Angela Duckworth explains that grit is innate tenacity. It's measured not by how you perform on a good day, but how you persist through a collection of bad days.

Grit thrives on the expectation that outcomes don't change overnight. Real mastery demands patience and the ability to delay gratification.

It might require a thousand quiet moments of practice for the one grand moment of performance. Learn to love the process, and to appreciate the incremental progress countered by the slower rhythm of mastery.

6.4. Tips to Foster Persistence

Fostering persistence is a recurring investment; no one-time deposit can guarantee lifelong returns. Establish SMART goals; goals that are Specific, Measurable, Attainable, Relevant, and Time-bound. This grounded approach anchors your efforts and provides a lucid assessment of your progress.

Brace yourself with resilience. Remember to bounce back, for you might fall seven times but stand up eight. Practice mindfulness, allowing yourself to take setbacks in stride, learning from them, and persistently marching ahead.

Remember, mastery is a celebration of the journey rather than the destination. The path to mastery is laden with tests of persistence, a test where defeat and triumph coexist. Nurturing persistence is like cultivating a carefully tended garden; water it with steady perseverance, prune it with resilience, nourish it with a positive mindset, and let grit be the sturdy roots grounding this extraordinary journey.

The art of persistence is a journey that brims with hard-won victories, remarkable learnings, bold encounters, and fascinating tales of resilience. It's a journey sown with dreams, watered with perseverance, and ripened under the sun of relentless hard work.

No matter what discipline you're poised for mastery, remember this: The ascent to greatness might be painstakingly slow, but the vista from the summit is unlike any other. It's the panoramic view of a journey marred yet beautified by persistent strides, echoing the victorious whispers, "I dared, I toiled, I persisted."

Chapter 7. In Tune With Your Talents: Exploiting Your Aptitudes

Life's virtuosos, the masters of their craft, often stand out not simply because of their inherent talent, but also due to their uncanny ability to discover their genuine strengths and maximize their potential. You too can penetrate the looking glass and uncover your hidden talents, honing them assiduously to ensure they serve you well.

7.1. Identifying Your Core Talents

Every individual is blessed with a unique set of abilities, aptitudes that singularly define their capabilities. It does not matter if the talents are conventional or unconventional, apparent or hidden; what does matter is their acknowledgment. To tap into your innate abilities, you must first delve into introspection, seeking personal awareness.

As you start your self-discovery journey, consider these key questions to unearth your talents:

- What are the activities that you naturally excel at?
- What do you do that brings you immense joy?
- When do you feel most fulfilled?
- What activities deeply engage you to the extent that you lose track of time?

Also, remember to link your talent's discovery to your life's broader perspective. How do these talents accentuate your passion, your purpose, and your overall vision of your life's grand direction?

7.2. Harnessing Your Talents to Your Advantage

Discovering your core talents is akin to unearthing precious stones. However, mere discovery does not suffice; the true value lies in their meaningful application, refining, and further enhancement. This requires a conscientious approach towards skill development and continuous learning, leading to maximum efficacy in utilizing your talents.

Stagnation is the bane of talent; hence, flexibility and openness to learn are the keys to unlock your talent's true potential. Seek mentors, absorb all available knowledge, challenge your limitations, and adopt a growth mindset that engenders personal and professional development.

Do not forget to respect the process. Talent mastery is a marathon, not a sprint. Patience, persistence, and practice are your stalwart companions on this journey.

7.3. Encouraging Your Individuality: The Differentiator

Recognizing your unique talents is empowering as it fosters individuality. Embrace your uniqueness and let it shape your journey. This will serve as your personal brand, your differentiating factor from the crowd. The world does not need more replicas; it hungers for authenticity, for voices that are daringly different yet thought-provoking.

Moreover, individuality is not incompatible with collective harmony. In fact, when a unique talent warmly resonates with shared goals, it aids in establishing strong connections, forging enriching relationships, and fostering camaraderie.

7.4. Aligning your Talents with Your Purpose and Vision

Having made an extensive study of your talents, the next step involves aligning them with your broader purpose and long-term vision. Investigate how your talents can fuel your passion, serve your cause, and aid in the realization of your dreams.

Your talents are your power, your arsenal - and when directed by vision, they become an unstoppable force contributing to your various pursuits, personal fulfillment, and an undeniable sense of achievement.

7.5. Bracing for Challenges and Roadblocks

The path to exploiting your talents and venturing into unfamiliar territories will subject you to challenges and roadblocks. This could be in the form of self-doubts, failures, criticism, or adverse circumstances. Instead of being disheartened by them, train yourself to absorb these blows and transform them into catalysts for growth.

Remember, failures are not the end, critics are not always right, rough patches are temporary, and doubts are a sign that you are pushing your boundaries and stepping outside of your comfort zone.

You are on a voyage of tremendous self-growth, exploring and tuning into your talents to reap maximum benefit. Make sure you cherish every part of this journey, revel in the process, learn from your experiences, and above all, never relinquish the belief in your capability to shine.

Chapter 8. The Balance of Life: Harmonizing Passion and Profession

The key to leading a fulfilling life lies largely in striking a harmonious balance between our passion and our profession. This delicate equilibrium helps us maintain a state of happiness, satisfaction, and stability while preventing the onset of burnout. Our journey will delve deeply into the importance of this balance, discuss tools to achieve it, and explore tangible steps to align passion and profession effectively. Doing so will ensure a dynamic life, brimming with joy, productivity, and success.

8.1. Unraveling the Dichotomy of Passion and Profession

In our modern world, we often find ourselves caught in a dichotomy, torn between following our heart's yearning - our passion, and conforming to societal norms and expectations - our profession. The societal model generally propagates a linear path, wherein one pursues an education, secures a job, and forges a career, often placing passion on the backburner. This model, while proven and followed, does not always breed satisfaction or happiness, and can sometimes lead to a sense of emptiness and lack of fulfillment.

Exploring the depth of this dichotomy requires us to comprehend passion and profession as separate entities. Passion, the driving force behind everyone's favorite pursuits, hobbies, and personal interests, instills a sense of joy, exhilaration, and satisfaction. On the other hand, choosing a profession, often dictated by the needs of the market and personal qualification, constitutes our work, career, and source of income.

8.2. Weaving Together Passion and Profession

The pivotal step towards harmonizing your passion and profession lies in acknowledging and understanding the unique value they both bring. Recognizing that they are not mutually exclusive but rather complementary components of your life can be transformative.

Consider your passion as the fuel that powers your journey through life. It instills a sense of wonder, elevates your spirit, and makes your life worthwhile. Your profession, in contrast, is the vehicle itself. It contributes to societal growth, ensures financial stability and progresses you towards tangible goals.

Drawing parallels between your passion and profession helps establish a common ground. You may find a way to develop your profession in line with your passion, or find a sector in your passionate field that has professional appeal. For instance, if your passion lies in painting and your profession in marketing, you can either derive marketing inspirations from your art or consider a role in an art gallery's marketing department.

8.3. Art of Prioritizing and Choosing Commitments

Prioritization plays an essential role in harmonizing passion and profession. Sometimes, this might mean prioritizing your professions during strict deadlines or crucial projects. Other times, your passion might need to take precedence. The choice and prioritization should be based on the individual circumstances at any given time.

Closing the gap between passion and profession requires consistent effort and adaptability. It might be necessary to hone additional skills or step out of one's comfort zone to align their passion and profession. This might mean taking an online course to improve your professional skills related to your passion or volunteering for projects that resonate with your passionate pursuits.

8.4. Coping With Challenges: Resilience and Adaptability

The intersection of passion and profession may not always be smooth and can be littered with challenges. Financial constraints, societal pressure, lack of support can be significant roadblocks, but resilience and adaptability can guide you through.

Being resilient gives you the strength to bounce back from setbacks and adapt to changes that come your way, while adaptability allows you to adjust your route, change direction, or alter your plan when circumstances demand. Adopting an open-minded and flexible approach can open horizons you never thought existed.

8.5. Sustaining the Balance

Harmonizing passion and profession is not a one-time task, and it demands continuous nurturing and sustenance. Regular check-ins can be beneficial where you sit down and reflect on if your passion and profession are in alignment and how you can improve this integration. Find a mentor or a coach who can provide an outside perspective and offer constructive feedback.

Remember, success is not just about fiscal achievements or professional milestones, but very much about how much joy, satisfaction, and personal growth you experience in your journey.

Striking a balance between passion and profession is much like orchestrating a symphony. Each note holds importance, yet it's the beautiful harmony they create as a whole that resonates deeply within the listener. Similarly, when passion and profession gracefully tango, you experience an enlightened existence that enriches every aspect of your life. As we journey on, remember this balance and strive towards it at every step, for it is here where true greatness lies.

Chapter 9. Networks of Support: Cultivating Beneficial Relationships

Human beings have thrived for centuries not because of individualistic prowess but because of shared knowledge, collaboration, and connection. It's in our very DNA to coexist in communities, deriving strength from shared resources and amplifying our potential through synergy. This chapter takes us through a comprehensive and thought-provoking exploration of the importance and nuances of creating and nurturing a robust network of profound connections, and its significance in the grand scheme of our journey toward self-actualization.

9.1. The Anatomy of Networks

When we speak of networks, it's not in terms of mere transactional, social media-based or professional acquaintances with whom you engage sporadically. Instead, imagine a network as a nurturing ecosystem of profound interpersonal relationships that serve to challenge, support, and inspire you as you strive to embrace your fullest potential. This intricate web of connections is comprised of mentors, teachers, friends, family, colleagues and various other individuals who directly or indirectly infuse positivity and growth into your life.

The deeper truth of networks surpasses the often commodified or transactional interpretation we accord to it. Networks are not about accumulating hundreds of LinkedIn connections or Facebook friends; it's about fostering an ecosystem that enables mutual growth and prosperity. It is a lively space of interchange where ideas, knowledge, experiences, strengths, and supports are shared, thus sculpting our personal and professional lives in more ways than we comprehend.

9.2. The Importance of Crafting Meaningful Relationships

Meaningful relationships are the cornerstones of a powerful network. Unlike superficial or fleeting interactions, these relationships are imbued with mutual respect, shared values, trust, emotional investment, and the unwavering desire to witness each other's growth.

These connections often summon a sense of belongingness and purpose in us, enlighten us with diverse perspectives, invigorate us with new learning experiences, offer a lifeline during turbulent phases, and, most significantly, inspire us by exemplifying the potential that can be tapped when passion is paired with perseverance.

Moreover, such relationships with diverse individuals can broaden our horizons and allow us to see life from various dimensions. This contrast of perspectives serves to enrich our understanding of the world, helping us to make informed decisions, stay resilient during setbacks, and grasp new opportunities that align with our journey toward self-discovery and growth.

9.3. Cultivating Beneficial Relationships: The Approach

Cultivating meaningful relationships necessitates time, effort, and insightful strategies. The following elucidation shines light on the vital aspects one ought to consider when building a resilient and supportive network of connections.

First, gravitate towards those who resonate with your values and aspirations. Such connections tend to be more fulfilling and less discordant.

Second, strive for reciprocity in all relationships. The ideal connections are those wherein there exists an equal give-and-take of kindness, support, knowledge, experiences, and inspiration.

Third, never underestimate the power of genuine appreciation. Be known as someone who praises openly and shares credit freely. This approach not only establishes a positive environment but also infuses deeper respect and trust in your relationships.

Finally, remember to be patient. Deep and meaningful relationships take their time to grow.

9.4. Nurturing the Network

Building a network of beneficial relationships is only the start. The real art lies in nurturing these relationships with consistent efforts, effective communication, unconditional support, and personal growth.

Prioritise the quality of interaction. Strive to add value and engage in ways that stimulate intellectual enrichment, emotional connectivity, and personal advancement. Regular communication, consistent empathy, mutual respect, appreciation, and shared experiences or learning sessions can stoke the fires of these relationships, ensuring they remain vigorous and enriching for all involved.

Remember, however, that nurturing relationships is not about compromising your journey or placating at every step. It's about harmonizing your personal journey with the growth and welfare of your network. It's about acknowledging interconnected growth. It's about realizing that while your fire alone can dispel darkness, together, the network's combined flames can usher in a brilliant dawn of transformative possibilities.

As you embark on this journey of cultivating beneficial relationships, bear in mind that this is not a one-time task but a life-long endeavor.

Meet it with empathy, patience, integrity, and the spirit of mutual growth, and watch as your network burgeons into a lustrous constellation of connections that lights your path toward your utmost potential and aids you in effectively seizing your greatness.

Chapter 10. Living Your Purpose: Transformative Actions

Behind every extraordinary story in history, the protagonist's purpose is consistently followed by transformative actions. These actions, fueled by desire and vision, have the ability to institute colossal changes. Movements are ignited, revolutions launch, and lives are completely transformed when individuals take the decisive step to act on their purpose. This chapter is dedicated to examining how you can turn your purpose into potent transformative actions that will shift your life's trajectory and propel you toward greatness. We will navigate through the fundamental principles of action, strategies for keeping momentum, and the role resilience plays in this transformative journey.

10.1. The Power of Action

Action is the catapult that launches you towards your dreams. It is the momentum that perpetuates motion towards the future you envision. Within every purpose-driven individual exists the potential for profound, impacting action. This potential, abundant and plentiful as it may be, remains dormant until stirred into awake by determined effort. However, understanding the necessity for action alone is inadequate; one must see the necessary steps as not merely tasks to be completed but as integral pieces of their journey towards self-realization.

Consider a situation where every day, the sun rises and shines brightly on a seed lying dormant within the soil. Its purpose is etched deep within its very core—to germinate, sprout, and evolve into a dainty flower or a robust tree. The intricate process can't be expedited, nor can it be circumvented; it requires persistent effort, patience, and resilience. Barring all environmental factors that could hamper its growth, if it weren't for the act of germination—the initial step towards its growth—the purpose contained within the seed would remain unfulfilled.

Likewise, your purpose is the seed that behooves your existence, and taking consistent action is the water and sunshine requisite for its growth. All transformative actions originate from personal purpose, bearing the potential to change the course of your life and affect those around you positively.

10.2. Strategies for Action

It's not enough to merely be aware of the need for action—one must build a framework to sustain consistent, purposeful activity.

1. Start Small: Venture into the unknown gradually with small steps. By starting small, you build confidence and create a safety net that enables you to bounce back when faced with challenges or failures.

2. Plan: Develop a roadmap of your journey. Knowing where to start and how to proceed can make the process less intimidating and more feasible.

3. Build Habits: Find ways to create new routines that align with your goal. These habits will become second nature, making ongoing action significantly easier.

4. Remain Adaptive: Flexibility and adaptability are key aspects to sustained action. Be willing and open to adjust your course as per the demands of your journey.

These strategies function as anchor points that foster continuous action, keep you grounded, and illuminate your path to actualizing your purpose.

10.3. Resilience and Action

In the face of adversity, two things can happen—one can either retreat or rise above the challenge. Resilience is what makes the latter possible. The transformative actions you embark upon may not always be straightforward. In fact, most of the time, they are wrought with obstacles and setbacks. It is during such times that resilience becomes instrumental.

Resilience encapsulates the ability to rebound from pitfalls, the tenacity to stand tall after being knocked down, and the endurance to keep moving forward irrespective of challenges. When risked against the vast ocean of uncertainty, even the sturdiest of ships are prone to occasional trembling. In life's metaphorical storm, resilience is your anchor; it prevents you from getting derailed from your purpose.

Your journey of living your purpose and translating it into transformative actions holds immense power. This power, once fully unveiled, can illuminate your life with meaning and impact, carrying you forward even amidst adversity. It's an explorative process that's continually evolving, pushing you towards your authentic self.

In essence, living your purpose is an odyssey. It is an enriching expedition that paints your life's canvas with vibrant shades of lessons, experiences, and breakthroughs. As each layer of purpose and related transformative actions unfurl, you gradually step towards becoming the best version of yourself. Not held back by the worries of yesterday, nor swayed by the uncertainties of tomorrow, you are entirely present in the moment, shining brightly in your world, one transformative action at a time.

Chapter 11. Your Legacy: Making a Lasting Impact

Legacy, it's often thought, is something we leave behind when we leave this world – footprints in the sands of time that echo our existence. But is it just about birth and death, or can it exist in the palpable present, shaping our actions and presence? Your legacy is a potent force - an enduring testament to the footprints you leave on the hearts and minds of others, recognized not just upon reflection after you're gone but in the real-time resonance of your actions. It is an fervent imprint, perpetually influencing others and leaving indelible traces on the tapestry of existence. Your legacy is defined by the impacts of your actions and, importantly, by your courage to dream and to create through your passion, purpose, and perseverance.

11.1. Crafting an Intentional Legacy

Firstly, legacy doesn't emerge exclusively from monumental contributions. It blossoms from everyday deeds, the smallest of acts sown with well intended thought. The consistency of your actions, attitudes, and decisions in everyday life contribute to the legacy you leave behind. Remembering this, it becomes essential to foster mindful living, ensuring that each act, no matter how small, resonates with your inner values and overall purpose. Stay faithful to your principles even when the journey becomes arduous. Stay vigilant about "right" actions. After all, it is not the intensity but the direction of the wind that determines the course of a sailing ship.

11.2. Leaving a Community Impact

The shape of your legacy profoundly impacts your community. Generosity, kindness, and empathy are the powerful triad that, when extended to others, reinforces communal bonds and creates a network of positivity. Remember that the legacy you leave is not merely about your personal achievements, but the way you cultivate inclusivity, nurturing community growth. A shared table has more laughter; consider this metaphor for all aspects of life.

11.3. Building a Lasting Impact Professionally

Think of figures like Steve Jobs or Ada Lovelace; they left tremendous legacies in their fields. However, you don't need to alter the course of humanity to forge a strong professional legacy. Striving to cultivate a supportive and creative work environment, consistently delivering quality work, or mentoring young enthusiasts in your field - all these contribute to your professional legacy. Let your life's work proudly carry your signature, even if only to remark "I made this, and I poured my heart and soul into it!"

11.4. Keeping the Lights On: The Legacy of Mentorship

A valuable aspect of building a lasting legacy is the power of mentorship. It gives you an opportunity to pass on your values, experiences, knowledge, and wisdom to others. A legacy of mentorship means guiding others towards their purpose while staying true to yours, connecting with mentees in a spirit of mutual growth. There is perhaps no greater testament to endurance than to witness your principles living on in others' lives.

11.5. Be a Life Learner: Evolving Your Legacy

Creating a legacy is an evolving process. Stagnation is a foe you don't want to embrace. The external world changes ceaselessly, and so must your inner world. Fostering a growth mindset, always seeking knowledge and new experiences, ensures that your legacy is dynamic and relevant. Your journey, like that of a river, should be marked by constant movement and a yearning for the boundless sea.

11.6. The Gift of Emotional Abundance: An Intangible Legacy

Lastly, remember that your emotional legacy is as essential as your tangible one. Radiate positivity, kindness, enthusiasm, and optimism across your interactions. Humans are emotional beings-at core, we remember how people made us feel. Be the person who brings joy into the lives of others, lighting up rooms and hearts alike with your emotional abundance.

In conclusion, your legacy is the sum total of your life's efforts, the imprints of your journey on the canvas of human existence. The making of your legacy is a life-long process, an orchestra playing out through your actions, attitudes, values, and contributions. It's not limited to the grand, sweeping events of your life, but is deeply embedded in the fabric of your everyday existence. From how you treat people to the values you uphold in challenging times, it is an empowering, enduring narrative - a testament to your journey, and crucially, an inspiration for others to seize their own greatness.